W9-ANF-526

FAR FROM ALGIERS

WICK POETRY FIRST BOOK SERIES
Maggie Anderson, Editor

Far from Algiers

Poems by

Djelloul Marbrook

The Kent State University Press

Kent, Ohio

© 2008 by Djelloul Marbrook
All rights reserved
Library of Congress Catalog Card Number 2008021129
ISBN 978-0-87338-987-7
Manufactured in the United States of America

The Wick Poetry Series is sponsored by the Stan and Tom Wick Poetry Center and the Department of English at Kent State University.

Library of Congress Cataloging-in-Publication Data
Marbrook, Djelloul.
    Far from Algiers : poems / by Djelloul Marbrook.
      p.   cm. — (Wick poetry first book series)
    ISBN 978-0-87338-987-7 (pbk. : alk. paper) ∞
    I. Title.
    PS3613.A7286F37 2008
    811'.6—dc22   2008021129

British Library Cataloging-in-Publication data are available.

12 11 10 09 08   5 4 3 2 1

for Marilyn

CONTENTS

ACKNOWLEDGMENTS

Acknowledgments are like funerals, notable for who isn't there, but those who must be mentioned are George B. Donus, David L. O'Melia, Rolfe Humphries, Alan Dugan, Stevie Smith, Wanda Ratliff, Raymond N. Nelson, Neild B. Oldham, David C. Wayland, David Gettman, Gail Godwin, Patricia L. Divine, Rosemary V. Klein, Martina Reisz Newberry, Amari Hamadene, Brent Robison, Wendy Klein, Dan Baum, Darya Marbrook Miller, George L. Wallace, Toi Derricotte, and Maggie Anderson.

The poem "Far from Algiers" was first published by *Arabesques Literary and Cultural Journal,* vol. 1, no. 2, November 2005.

What a joy to find that the "emerging" first book poet I had chosen for the Stan and Tom Wick Poetry Prize is a journalist, a man 73 years old who had published poems "in his youth." How honored I am—how lucky—to have been able to choose this superb first book by Djelloul Marbrook that honors a lifetime of hidden achievement. It has also been an amazing pleasure to find out from his website about his deep concern and lifelong advocacy for women's rights.

How does a reader (me) sense in the poet—though it is never spelled out in his poems—the person inside of the poems, the man who speaks from his life, too, to her heart? I have always thought that a great poem is an imprint of the poet's mind. Through it we see deep down to the center. When I read these outspoken concerns in his essays, I admired his poems even more, for the way they embody and speak these passions at the deepest level while, at the surface, they give us a language that broaches both eastern and western poetic traditions and reveals a voice that belongs to the vulnerable and exiled part of us all.

There were several top manuscripts. I went back to read them many times. I noticed, during this final process, that I felt the desire not only to read *Far from Algiers* again and again but to read Algerian history. I wanted to dredge the metaphor. The poems are seductive like that; they hold many layers. They make the mind want to participate. One reads along, then a line drops you to an under floor. Sometimes the poems seem utterly symbolic, surreal; they are philosophical, historical, psychological, political, and spiritual. The genius is in the many ways these poems can be read. I kept being rewarded by new awarenesses of the poet's intentions, by the breadth and scope of the manuscript.

As I read, I felt more and more that it was impossible that this was a first book. It seemed the writer knew exactly what to say and, more importantly, exactly what to leave out. His skills and insight make this book seem a book written after many others. I am drawn back to mysteries: Who is speaking? Is it an autobiographical voice? The voice of an everyman? But the voice is "foreign" to me, and, this time, by that I mean wonderful—I mean that it is original.

1

CLIMATE CONTROL

Stuff the mailboxes and night repositories
against my attempts to insert
flat evidence of my belonging here.

I'm as sick of wanting to get in
as I am of wanting to be heard.
I was born with one of those faces that say

Trust me, you don't want to hear it.
Bad enough listening to myself,
who needs you to confirm the news?

My climate's not suitable for growing
the fruit expected of your tree
and I see you have no patience for experiment.

I've misunderstood great men in useful ways
in the natural course of an alien life,
so why would I quarrel with locked doors?

BITCHY NURSE

(Algiers, August 12, 1934)

If I'm not talking to you,
if this isn't how I talk to me,
that leaves the little bastard
who started tagging along
after my cold welcome in Algiers.

The French nurse bitched
the kid needed milk and a name.
A little welcome would be nice,
but she kept that to herself
because they were distracted

by the opera of themselves,
the cliché the three of them
had painted on the world,
red and squawking graffiti
never meant to be foreground.

That's the cast, everyone else
is an understudy bound
by the uninspired script.
I don't encourage them because
I've heard what they have to say.

But you, you're different,
listening as if someone
has something to say.

DJELLOUL

What kind of a name is that?
I invite you to notice *that*
is the sound of deportation.

My name is not contagious.
Is quarantine necessary?
Wouldn't exile be better?

I remember I'm from nowhere
but a spurt in thoughtless dark:
you've nowhere to send me.

It's French, I could say. Who knows
the difference? The difference is that
it's Arabic with French panache.

Jeh-lool, go on, try it.
Terrorists bear the name, scientists
and singers, and a few cashiers

can even say it without help
because they've turned their battlements
into condominia of hope.

    What kind of name is that?
The name of a Saracen lancer
ghosting in the dusk of Provence
and the name of a citizen deported
a thousand times a year.

FAR FROM ALGIERS

An unnamed race slips by
ethnographer and xenophobe,
roiling bowels and hackles,
electrifying space.

Genomes tell us nothing
about our overlords;
we know we're an underclass
to these corsairs and otherlings.

They break our doors at night,
take our wives and children,
foul our consensus with ideas
and scat full sail on glassy seas.

Though we take them to our beds
they're unwelcome in our churches;
they profane our certainties
and stir up gifts renounced.

South of every guarded circle
is a Barbary where our rules
stand on their heads and dance
to tunes of turbans and scimitars.

Their ships fly no flags until
it's far too late and we're engaged
in the kind of bloodiness youth
prays for to spite the social good.

Every simpleminded day
guards against kidnappers,
every complacency has its *dey*
fat on ransom in some Algiers.

If there were no Barbary Coast
to haunt our dreams and genes
we'd eat potatoes, bed our cousins
and be as stupid as we want to be.

TROUBLED BOY

A boy who looks embarrassed to be young
skulks beneath the scaffolds avoiding light:
I hope I will not have to be his like again:
he glances up at me and remembers being old.
No other bond is as strong as this.

AUTOBIOGRAPHY

They were pussyfooting, so I disowned me for them.
The hospital insisted they give me a name
and suggested a little milk with it.

Somebody else had been born, someone
I didn't know and never would want to know.
If Algiers felt like the wrong place, so would everywhere else.

If you're born to meet the wrong people, Algiers
is as good as any place to start, and in 1934
even better if there was any doubt about where you belong.

I left the little bastard and never looked back.
What became of him had nothing to do with me
nor with anyone else involved in the project.

I don't know what the French did with him.
God knows how they peeled off his shadow.
I took mine with me, figuring it would come in handy

for darkening threatening doorsteps.
I could tell from the start it would be messy and dramatic—
my father and his two lovers looking down on me glumly.

Heartache was more welcome than I was.
Under the circumstances I felt it prudent
to relieve the principals of the burden of disowning me,

but there remained the question of where to put me,
so once again I beat them to the punch:
the safest place was clearly in harm's way.

There my father, coming to his senses, could come to find me.
He never did, but late in life I found his child
cowering in a corner and picked him up and calmed him.

THE FLUTES OF THE DJINN

I don't know, djinn, how much you remember
but I know you measure the Sahara's sands,
wear stars on your fingers
and remember that once on Third Avenue
an old man freed you and asked nothing.
You studied him a long time before you left
to make sure he understood the consequences.
He did. And then he left,
and somewhere a child was born
wearing them on his face.

How do their flutes in the Tuareg night
summon us to the secrets of the djinn,
and how does the sexual electric of stars
wake us to the meanness of our wishes?
I think hearing is easier than seeing them
thanks to our brushes with the vast.
Abhor the misshapenness of words
and make this gnosis your heart:
everything is a facet of the same jewel.

SINISTRAL

And what is your background?
I have an advanced degree in bastardy.
Excuse me, I'm not familiar . . .
Of course you're not, there's no excuse.

I am a highly skilled outsider,
learned even. Nothing can shake me
from my resolve to leave
or my distrust of doors.

There is only my djinni to lead me
through the loud exhibitionism of the world.
Only my djinni affirms
groups are to keep us out.

Being born somebody's bastard
made me everyone's. I went
about the work of finding
the idea of belonging strange.

I am to the left of belonging,
forlorn, bereft and looking in.
Some are conceived under stars,
I was conceived under stairs.

You asked what my background is.
I wish I had one, but if I did
I would probably know less than I do
and be more certain about it.

THE MEMORY OF SAND

She crosses minds and rents lockers
but never properly lives anywhere
because her nature is to be Arabia
and certain configurations subject
to wind, inherent lawlessness
and the seductions of the djinn.

And if her crossings are trackless
they do leave swamp gas in blasted eyes
and the fragrance of recent encampments
in a desert always threatening
the wells of verdant enterprise.
She is the memory of sand.

SUBMARINE

When I reached the counter
the clerk looked behind me.

All a floor could be relied on
was to tip and turn to ice.

When I saw familiar faces
they saw someone else.

It's better to be invisible
than inconvenient,

the latter having no advantages.
I thought it would help to make reports,

but it seems that requires a home.
I was the least thing I'd forgotten.

No one waited for me,
no one regretted leaving,

but there were few regrets
I didn't manage to entertain.

My wake is smaller
than a periscope's.

Nothing ever happened
that couldn't without me.

Some would call it a Sufi life
if it had won their attention.

That's not what submarines do.

Real wars are fought at home;
historic wars reflect them.

I destroyed enough by accident;
I didn't need orders to confuse me.

STRONGBOX

What's hidden hums
from the back of things
behind boxes and faces,
low current in the pleats
of stories we've hung up.

I dowse for resources
quickening in the dark.
Sucker punches bruise my heart
when I slip around to the back,

that's how I know I'm hot.
Everywhere there's facade
the street signs are turned around
and in such beguiling places.

True home is through enemy lines,
true enemies pose as friends.
Whoever's selling nothing
is a truly frightening man.
I hope you've met one lately.

WHAT GOOD DID MY OWN GOOD DO ME?

It wasn't those who said they did
who had my good in mind.

Maybe I thought within a great within
were the grandeurs of the cosmos, or
one little secret might clothe me better
through thorny meetings I'd forgotten.

Success came cheap to those
who, looking after me, didn't look at all.
Who wished us less than freedom
gave us faith and apocalypse.

Threats of bad acting stopped
my too respectful mouth.
I knew I had a fatal crack;
I squirmed away from touch.

PORT OF ENTRY

I imagine death an empty place
where we get used to what we've got
and put on what we knew all along.

My guess is we can't get our names
past immigration, much less
all we've pretended to be.

I sleep these days smiling to think
how we'll fly in that lightened state
needing no papers, being beyond words.

THE ANGEL DEPARTS

Now every creak and whimper of light
molests me in an ancient bed,

I remember sending myself away
and staying here without a name

to follow the leads of movie actors,
to pretend to live the life others

say I lead, but to know I'm gone
and to hope I've gone somewhere

truth is not an intrusion
on the ordinariness of our lives.

We didn't say good-bye because
some horrors are a long time sinking in.

I never asked myself who
stayed on to playact here,

to hear the moments' rain
but not to feel except

cold unwelcome tampering.
When the angel had gone, leaving

this shiverer to contend with sores
that would never heal, and lies

that blinded me, I was glad
to spare him.

UNDER THE GRATES

When I was young I didn't have the sort of face
men of consequence cotton to,
but the desolate studied me
in subway cars. I hear their heartbeats now
under the grates. I remember their faces.
I think I have kept faith with them,
but I would be hard put to tell them how.

The professors had a great deal to say,
saying nothing the desolate said more.
My bones were their tuning fork.

Then there were the inevitables
who lost themselves disliking me;
among them count lovers and my mother.
I think of them with a sob and permanent dismay.

FAMILIARITY

I know no one,
no one knows me.

There in that limbo
I live precariously.

THE GREAT GAME

I'm always in two countries at once,
the one where you say I am
and the one where I know I am.

Travel is becoming difficult
owing to the terrorist threat
and currency problems.

Unification seems unlikely
because of cultural differences
and the usual language problems.

Besides, I suspect your motives.
After all, I live well in my head
but must step lightly in yours.

GHOSTS

The tribe inhabiting your face
remembers an ancient feud with me,
but its envoys pretend we've just met.

I would rather my own face teem
with the cities whose streets I've walked
and lovers who nurse no quarrels with me.

MY SHIP COMES IN

What will they do with their grievances
    where they've gone?
They have no need of them so
    they come back for mine
and take them in the places that I dream
    knowing I don't recognize my benefactors.

They crowd around me as my hair falls out.

Their forgivenesses are rock roses
    descending to the black river
    where the final boat
    is loaded with things I never did.

Is it true, God, you and I co-operate the world?

Bless them, bless them where they've gone.

Is it true, God, dreams tell us something of your mind?

Bless us, bless us where we choose to go.

Boxes full of moments that arrested us
    are put aboard the boat,
    my treasures which I intend to pass
    with your permission, God,
    through customs between the worlds.

I plan to live there resting and alert
    to the few who brush aside the veil
    yet fail to see nothing looks different.

OLD CHARTS, WARM RAIN

1

We used to be able to drop off the edge;
now the best we can do is hang our feet over it
imagining warm rain lulling us to dream
of floating barefoot in vaguely familiar cities,
handicapped by words, wondering why mysteries
that dogged us in another life seem obvious.

2

When I dream warm rain falling on my feet
only the blind will see my face
and I will never need to eat again,
words slide out of reach and finally
I dial me down and go through walls
to get to the other side of things.

3

We suffered loss deciding the world is round
needing as we do to flirt with precipice.
I keep the old charts in my head, I know
where there be dragons to feed
delicious caravels captained by corsairs
tormenting lovely slaves. I can drift off
this grinding round of gravity
to cast myself loose among my fears.

4

Dragons send me polite communiqués,
pointing out this and that in deference
to my concern for their good health,
but I don't try to pass their gifts
for wisdom, I'm just a go-between.
My caul is nailed up in the pilot house;
it didn't bring me any luck.

VAN GOGH'S DRAWINGS

(Metropolitan Museum of Art, December 2005)

1

A fit of sun broke off,
somehow got in his blood,
banged inside his skull.

You can see it: in 1889
he drew it like a gong
working wheat to climax.

Black chalk, brown ink,
pink paper, no one
could survive this sun,

but for a year he did:
seventy-five paintings,
fifty drawings, and then

too bright, too loud, too close,
the world demanded
to be brought to an end.

2

I move right to left
countering wont of words,
their murmurous readers,
studying his reed strokes.

So it's been, upstream
to spawn unlikely ideas,
but why him to show me
my contrarian spite?

The sane envy the blind:
if you see that, the ozone
vanishes and the sun
beats your brains out.

THE MEN'S ROOM

Twenty of me in a mirrored room
don't figure to get through the night,
all their Etruscan heads teetering
on mortuarial bodies.
Something's worrying them,
an echo seen from the corner
of a stranger's eye, and stranger
is the iteration of a madness
not seen in the original. In fact,
the original must be posited
in the middle of a psychotic break.
Maybe the lemon-curried shrimp
accounts somehow for the disappearance
of a man so full of himself
at first he thought the world
needed twenty more of him,
but then he realized he'd been divided
into twenty saddened parts.

RESPITE

You can spend your life overcoming your face
which only hardens its cast.

The sculptor not the sculpture needs
a diplomatic visa from your eyes.

I've never worried about his face
so malleable to others' light;
it only occasionally visits me,

telling me about frisking women
for hidden jewels, demanding tribute
from the panjandrums of Cockaigne.

CURTAINS

Houses war to keep
what happens in them
from suck and blanch
of time. This much I know,
but what's the meaning
of my homeyness in them,
places I couldn't have been,
lives I couldn't have lived?
Torn curtains blowing
from blasted houses stop
my breath and remind me
of what I couldn't have felt
      or thought or done.

CATALYSIS

Back to algae,   sough of clouds,
wondering if   cognitions lighten me
or curse my blood   with grief.
Water's my estate,   moods of heavens
draw my faces,   mend my clothes.
My days lugging   memories around
dissolve in thanks of light on ponds.

PAROLE VIOLATOR

I am ready,
I have been reunited with all my pens;
now nothing is too bright, too loud, too big.
Mighty disorders in my head prepare
for cavity searches and branding looks
prod me to savage lockdowns in my skin.

I am ready
for the failure of disguise, the barge
of things formerly held to scale
and emergence of people as their imaginings.
But should I fail to choose them carefully
words will hand me over to omnivores.

AMBITION

I've settled in my skin.
I get around my bones,
but I'm never at home.

I'd like the moment's rest
of being who I say I am,
of letting it go at that,

not obtruding, lurking
or expecting, an eleven o'clock
shadow of the unforlorn.

DANGER

Some days toothbrushes turn strange,
nothing can be trusted to be
as it was. Back doors and gloves
repel, fond items belong
to people no longer friends
and by some small shift this,
this place murmurs otherness
and has the low glow of danger.

THE PRICE OF CRUDE

If I weren't working in the dark
life wouldn't be half so interesting;
I'd have to study the barrel cost
of light sweet crude resentment
as if there were an algorithm,
like testing proven reserves,
instead of frolic in a mysterium.

I see the red air tremble when
epithelials are feeding roses;
nothing is more irreducible
than anger poured upon our wake
and if it ever were to run out
how would we gin up wars
and molest the child within?

THE PRICE OF ADMISSION

Give me members, I'll give you distrust,
except perhaps for body parts,
because of who's willed out.

Give me members, I'll give you grief,
parts conspiring against the whole
in definition of disease.

I don't want to belong
to any group that would have me
because of all whom I would betray.

What excludes sooner or later kills
and in the ever-narrowing space
many catch their deaths of cold.

Give me members, I'll give you war,
the absence of anything better to do
in fear of a world left out.

ONENESS

I tried following you through the glass wall
but I'm not ready for such elegance.
I wish you wouldn't tempt me.
I must have thought for a second
we'd become one as I've hoped.

It's earned me a broken nose.
But it's a small price to pay
for such lovely confidence.
I'm sure I'll try again.
We started out impossibly apart,

you being the very emissary of God.
I think our distance has been closed.
I should have used my subtler gifts
such as taking in an entire room,
but I wanted something unexplained,

something that would finally prove
what our conversation meant.
I'm ashamed of this lapse. Forgive me.
I should know what passes through glass
is the desperate oneness of desire.

PROFANITY

The pleasure of saying thank you
is outweighed only by welcomes
we don't hear or see because
they're so numinously everywhere.

This so distracted the Greeks
they put gods where they could see them
and even painted on their faces
so fixed they were on form.

Arabs thought this containment
a profanity so profound
they bore the zero out of India
to spin the cosmos in its circuit.

The treasure of saying thank you
is the magic it sets in motion
and all we have to do is know
we're the gods we're arguing about.

SECOND MOSES

Moses de Leon peddled glories   on street corners
copies of an ancient rabbi's work he said   I think of him
when I think of books   hawking Zohar bit by bit
I think how greed   is shaming written words
how all of us with nothing to say   are clamoring
to say it exorbitantly   there was no way to claim it
once he'd written it   it rose and soared and
turning to go home   he died
as he might have written that he should

THE FLAVOR OF LIES

Who's thinking of you now?
Your name slips her mind
but you still offend her.

Can you imagine the lives
we're living in peoples' heads?
Oh yes, you're afraid you can.

And to think this, like androgyny,
is a birthright sold for salt
to flavor parents' lies.

3

A FITTING PLACE

I'm nostalgic for where I'm not
and sometimes have never been:
Granadan windows, battlements,
places of which strangers smell—
born nostalgic as if here
had been a mistake, born
by mistake and so disoriented
everything would be strange
until I'm somewhere stranger.
I don't think my genes
entertain the same nostalgias
but on this they do agree:
this is not the place, you
are not the one, and I am not
here, there or between,
but in a hell of a bad fit.

COMMONEST WORD

A life is filled with just so many accidents
and it looks as if mine are running out.

There's so little left
there's a kind of breathlessness,
a gasping toward the end.

I like this feeling better
than all the spendthrift hoarding earlier.

I think it's as close as I'm going to get
to any kind of settlement
between the halves I've tried to reconcile
this long brutalizing while.

God in me that's always saying yes
is picking up her radiances to go
and leave me here in the dark
where the commonest word is no.

THE AIR ABOUT HIM IS TOO THIN

The man who darkens faces blessing him
dresses in his sorrows well. He pretends
he hears only what we speak. Even then
he edits subtler punctuations out.
Not a man whose funeral we'll attend
and yet one in whom we briefly hoped.

Shower him with your belongings,
still everywhere he half belongs.
Much as you coveted it you will gasp
in the thin air of his eye, you will grope
for handholds in the face of his reserve,
descending to a phantom street.

HURRICANE SPAGHETTI

Waiting for a hurricane   is like growing up
or growing old,   you don't have a clue
what's happening,   but whatever it is,
you don't have enough insurance to cover it.

Possible routes   called spaghetti,
colors and categories   are all laid out
in a cornucopia   of possibilities,
invitations to orgies of impendingness.

The special sorrow   of waiting for one
is being reminded   we're always waiting
for something to happen   and when it does
we'll be no more than its flotsam.

NO GOOD-BYE

We split up to confuse the dogs.
Never had time to say good-bye.
I hear he's a game fall guy.

And nothing ever happened to me again.
I slid far from everyone's reach
to observe the bastard who had been me.

Now that shit happens to someone else
I see that the one the dogs run down
is the one whose heart smells best.

AND SO MY PHARAONIC HEAD

They don't know what to make of me. Condolences.
Pharaonic head, headlight gaze: indigestion.
Flatheads, horseheads, profilers choke
on this specter from medieval courts. Ciao, baby,
salaam alaikum too, and regards to your digestive tract.

I eat lightly these days, having had to stomach a lot.
Free trade and tribalism, hot damn. Religion's
poor antacid, but what else is there in view
of our unfortunate habit of dying? I don't know
what to make of them, either. My regrets,

but I will be unable to attend whatever you have in mind.
I arrived here with prior commitments which
just now I remember, and as there is very little time left
I must be about the business of putting my ardors away
and for the last time fondling the allures of this place.

EXILE

(Juanita Guccione, 1904–1999)

Even toasters defeated her,
but you couldn't imagine my mother
holding a brush or palette knife
uncertainly or in repose.

She painted as if she knew the number
of each brush's hairs, number, wont, complaint—
intimacies that seduced her.

Headiness of varnishes and turps,
unctuousness of cadmium,
the asperity of her own gaze
made her expatriate in her skin.

Her world was nothing but her studio
and one of her materials eternity.

DREAD COMMERCE

Block my words or path, revile
something in this face communing
with angels unwelcome in your life.

I know what commerce deranges you
between a man and the lives he's lived.
I'm the very person you need to meet

And I no more wish to know you
than you me, but we should at least ask
why we've had this mean encounter.

As for your rudeness, perhaps it's not as great
as mine in seeming I have something to say
or, worse, somewhere important to go.

A SIXTY-BAG DEPARTURE

Some day your life is ending up in thirty-gallon bags
on the street, and the rest of it will be shipped
in boxes to people who think it's overdue.

Think of stone faces of Stoics laughing in museums.
Hold that thought when they pull the plug
and you flatline to your debriefing.

I figure you for sixty bags and thirty boxes
and hanging around just long enough
to make sure nobody's jumping up and down.

You won't be looking for me when you come back,
shared blood having always made us invisible to each other,
so when I hear you laugh that will suffice to make us free.

ESCAPE ROUTE

We must go out of our minds
or we'd kill ourselves in them.
Here is my escape route:

a Moorish garden in al-Andalus
where an old man is watching
aspens write on walls.

Shuddering aspens draw a pall
across white tiles, and his mind
plummets to its death in sleep.

Only the aspens' shadows can
lure him over this precipice.
Otherwise he's a lunatic

trapped in his skull and raving,
desperate to become a particle
in some grand project of light.

Sleep, that fathomable sea
and petri dish of the cosmos,
I assign your debt to aspen leaves.

WHAT A PLACE

Somewhere between cliché and adage
and under a foot of snow
I fell down, cried and froze to death.

It was one thing to hear lightning
break off the past, another
to think I'd never see it again.

Heaven didn't interest me very much;
I was trying to imagine a place
where there would be nothing to say,

no getting lost or loss.
It was better than soiled fantasy
even if I had to start to finish.

If they don't file me in that truck,
if I only rest, I'm glad the snow has covered
the backwardness of my going forth.

HASAN IBN AL-SABAH

(Lord of the assassins, 11th century)

Exile is a twofold problem:
no one eludes it and
mourned land disappears.

So while I hoped to complain,
I've nothing to complain about
except the poignant delusion

that some of us belong and
must be vigilant for those
who live among us in disguise.

We need the assassins
to exonerate what we do,
to make it seem less awful.

Hasan ibn al-Sabah lives
in our churches on Sunday,
in mosques and synagogues.

We can't describe his face
because we wear it while
we hunt the foreign devils.